impressions
A WRITING ANTHOLOGY 2018

THURSDAY
OCTOBER 25
10:00am – 8:00pm

FRIDAY
OCTOBER 26
10:00am – 8:00pm

SATURDAY
OCTOBER 27
10:00am – 4:00pm

THE GREAT HALL | 180 E 5TH STREET | ST. PAUL, MN 55101

artability

PEOPLE
INCORPORATED

PeopleIncorporated.org | 651.774.0011

TABLE OF CONTENTS

Perish with this
Hallowed Declaration
Locked in
My Soul,
I would Surely Die Twice.

Because,
I have Waited
So Long.
Eons,
Eternity,
Infinity,
It Seems,
To Touch Your Cheek
And Say,
"I love you...."

Poetry

To let the
Divine Syllables,
Chained like
Innocent Prisoners in my
Lungs,
Out.
Not in a
Mad Escape,
But in
Righteous Exoneration.
These Sacred Words
Constrained in
Chains of Fear,
Longing to see the
Light of Day, and
Herald the
Secret They Keep.

This Hidden Proclamation
That Once Released Can never be
Imprisoned Again.
Justly or Otherwise.

There is this
Painful Sense of Safety in My
Sorrowful Self-Censorship.
Because I do not know if
The Heavens will rejoice as
A Song of an Angelic Chorus
Reverberates of off the Stars and Planets
Once this Hidden Knowledge is
Revealed, or if it will be the
Gates of Hell
Flung Open, and the
Demons of Humiliation and Rejection
Crawl the
Earth at
The Expense of
My Emotional Welfare.

Alone and covered in its own stench!
Or a fever induced hallucination
Leaving me
Choked by delusions and disappointment?

This isn't real.
This can't be happening.

A sudden increase of passion's intimate cadence
Leads to an implosion
As all of my senses collide
Then explode like a nova.
I am lost.
I don't exist.
I am surrounded by eternity and ecstasy.

This isn't real.
This can't be happening.

Her breath slows.
I open my eyes
Placing my forehead on hers,
Our souls wave at each other
Through our eyes.
The tips of our noses touch.
I inhale as she exhales.
My lungs fill with
Her breath.
Sweet and newly released.
Grins slide across our faces
In unison.

This is real.
This is happening.

Because I've always known Heaven existed.
And this is Paradise.

Lips parted slightly.

This isn't real.
This can't be happening.

I can barely tell
Her eyes open.
She smiles now.
No question.
Her delicate hand reaches up.
Fingernails slide down
The center of my neck to my shoulders.
Slowly her hand opens
Then closes at the base of my skull. Pulling me to her.

This isn't real.
This can't be happening.

Our lips meet.
Soft and passionate.
Like a shadow meeting the sun.
Mouths open faintly.
Searching each other with our tongues
With the delicacy of New explorers.

This isn't real. This can't be happening.

The engine of her chest beneath me.
Its percussion driven symphony
Reverberating into my essence.
Moving to her sleek neck
Soft, faint kisses are
Responded to by
A staccato of
Warm bursts of breath
In my ear.
Teeth clasp onto its lobe.

This isn't real.
This can't be happening.

How do I not know
I will awaken
Like a schoolboy

2018 Writing Artists

DAVID LLOYD BEEBE

BERSERKER
Nonfiction

On Saturday, May 9, 1987 (the day before Mothers' Day), Arden is admitting me to the lockup psych station. I am being difficult. He snaps at me and hurts my feelings. Just like my Dad, Arden snaps at me. He hurts my feelings.

The next day Arden is standing behind the nurses' desk. I fall down on the carpet and take aim and fire an "air" sniper rifle at Arden.

Shortly thereafter I "realize" the hospital is on fire and we are all going to die. "Fire," I yell, "fire." And I walk back to an empty room. Arden follows me. We are alone in an empty room and I am shouting, "fire."

Arden has done this and viciously, savagely, I turn on him. I'm going to beat the shit out of him before we all die.

I twist his arm behind his back. He says, "You're breaking my arm," and for some reason I let him go. We wrestle to the floor and I try to pull out his gold earring. The emergency squad arrives. Eight big guys surround me. I think they're going to kill me. I shout, "I'm mentally ill! I'm mentally ill!" I thought they were going to kill me.

They don't kill me – they put me in 4 points – for three days.

On the third day the staff ask me if I want to see my friend Dawn. When Dawn comes, she says, "You could have told me you were tied up."

LOVE AND COMMITMENT
Nonfiction

I pilfer two bowls from the kitchen and put them on a table in the dayroom. This is Station 60 – general clinical psychiatry at University of Minnesota Hospitals. I open two cartons of Marlboro's and put the packs in one bowl. I open two cartons of Newport's and put the packs in the other bowl.

I put a sign – not a concept – in front of the two bowls: FREE.
(Become a Marlboro man and travel to a new port.)

KAREN WOOD

ENJOY YOUR FATE
Poetry

Sometimes a plan, and the outcome take their own beautiful direction. Then it's time for the artist to sit back and observe where fate takes each person. It is so beautiful. Enjoy your fate. Thank you.

GLENN WM. WYMORE

HER EYES APRIL 24, 2018
Poetry

Her eyes frightened him.

Not because he got lost in them.
Although he did,
But it wasn't the kind of lost
One feared.
It was being lost in wonder and marvel.

It wasn't because they were deep and mysterious,
Like a midnight lake.
For they also glimmered
Like the stars upon the still waters.

Those eyes scared him,
Because in them
He saw something
He thought he'd
Never see again.

Himself smiling.

UNREAL HAPPENING
Poetry

This isn't real.
This can't be happening.

I open my eyes and see her.
A smile not a smile across her
Resplendent face, draped in moonlight.

desk and covered them with a sheet. The result looked something like a coffin and something like a baby carriage.

My commitment hearing was coming up. Thursday, May 16, 1974 at 10 AM. (Tomorrow.) The staff insisted it was a "hearing" but I called it a "trial" – a "try all." "Try all" ways to capture my soul.

I met with my attorney. I told him, "I have a list of so people I want subpoenaed. They will testify to my sanity. I am not incompetent!" My attorney said, "I will do the right thing."

After meeting with my attorney, I call Sandy on the phone. I ask her to testify at the trial. She says she will. She asks me who I am. I tell her I am the Northwestern Bell Central Operator. She tells me she has been having trouble with her phone. She tells me to knock it off.

All in all, I am frightened. The try all was frightening. I had been wearing a blue denim suit. I take it off and put it in between the mattress and the box spring of my bed. That blue denim suit was the real me. I was now on the periphery and the suit was my center. Nothing that happened to me on the periphery would affect my center.

At nine that Thursday morning I went into the bathroom of a vacant room. I lit a candle and some incense and put them in the shower. (Candles and incense were prohibited on the unit.) This was my central self – my Atman.

The trial begins.

I say, "I have no special powers but the power to act as I do."
Sandy asks the judge, "Why do you have a video camera behind the mirror on the wall?"

I ask Gert – the social worker – to leave the courtroom. (Gert is girt with sombrero earrings.) (Get out!)

When Gert leaves the room, I do too. I check the candles and the incense. I check the blue denim suit. I pray. When I go back to the courtroom the try all is over.

"The county judge
He held a grudge
But we never will be found...
Band on the run."
I never will be found...but...
I AM COMMITTED.

DUSK
Fiction

.... W a l l s melt away as eyes are closed,
.... birds continue to sing
.... S T A R L I G H T ~~~/~~~ continues to shine
.... trees rock __/ __ to and fro as the wind blows.

LACEY WOIDA

PAPER GARDEN
Poetry

Maybe my pen and my paper are becoming safe ground.
Maybe if I plant words in between the lines and let the ink soak in something beautiful might grow.

THE GREATEST ROMANCE
Poetry

Perhaps writing will be the greatest romance for me. Maybe the greatest chase is that between my ink-filled pen and the blank pages of an open book. It is in paper's nature to hold great reservoirs of torrential ink between its pages. Never drying up and always beckoning for more. The bound paper fears no commitment and knows nothing of being smothered. It welcomes every day at any hour, my passion, my sorrows, and my insights, it can contain it all. Gladly it gives up its pages to be filled with the mystery of the paradox that lies between weakness and strength. Open to search out the simplistic yet complex nature of romance, beauty, love, and truth. The many pages gladly give up the secrets of the writer to each new passing eye. It's a place where strangers can wade through the deluge of ink and draw from them the words they need at the time they need it.

VAPOR
Poetry

She feels unreal detached like a vapor forced to serve a life sentence of endless drifting till one day she simply vanishes into thin air.

Nonfiction

I'm in seclusion. I'm in the quiet room. It's empty. There is silence.

But I can make music. I'm a one-man-band. I'm "the band" on the "run." I'm a drummer. And I have my percussion instruments.

I pound on the bathroom door. (It is locked.) Ka Boom. Ka Boom. Ka Boom. I drum on the security screens. Ratata, Ratata. I jiggle the handle on the locker. (Here, kitty, Hear, Kitty.) And then I smash the locker door, Carash, Carash. (Take that kitty.) Jiggle, jiggle, jiggle. Carash, carash! I pound on the outside door. Ka Boom, Ka Boom, Ka Boom.

The staff hears me and doesn't realize its music. They think I'm on a rampage.

* * *

The staff put me in 4 points. I'm paranoid as all hell and they make me HELPLESS.

* * *

In my HELPLESS state incantations come to me. The sun is shining in the windows of the quiet room. The sun light is in my eyes. I believe I am wearing sunglasses to hide the light shining from my eyes. I say out loud. "Pull down the shades, there is light in my eyes." (Pull down the window shades, pull down the sunglasses.)

(The sunlight is in my eyes. The light is shining from my eyes.)

And then I speak out loud another incantation. "I'll never marry." (I will remain single.) "I'll never marry." (I will not be a minister and marry couples.) And "I'll never, marry." (I won't jump your bones.)

I'm all tied up and I'm thinking in knots.

I'm suddenly very tired. I fall asleep.

DOUGLAS BLUE

BEYOND ME
Poetry

Above my solitude
My sand
Beyond my shores teased by faithless waves

Nonfiction

Your brain got stuck.
You could find no luck.
Life seemed unbearable.
Not wanting to hurt anyone, you felt no options.
You were untreated for what others could not see.
In a brief moment of insanity, you took your own life.
You seemed fine, no warning sign.
Your brain was stuck, like in a rut.
Always with a smile, you fooled us.
In shock you left so many.
We did not know you could find no peace.
You could not move forward, peace was not around.
Your pain just moved, transferred to the one's left behind now.
No one is to blame.
There should be no shame.
No one knew your brain was stuck.

MARY VORHES

FLITTING ABOUT
Poetry

Color in the air
Butterflies flitting about
Beautiful to see.

FLYING BY
Poetry

Herons flying by
On Mississippi river
What a sight to see.

IN FULL BEAUTY
Poetry

Yellow, orange, red Daffodil,
tulips and more
Spring in full beauty

because we are so self-consumed nowadays with self-gratification that we can't see past the mirror. Look at the whole picture in the whole situation.

TERRI TERESA

LIVING WITHOUT YOU
Nonfiction

This we wanted to yell scream and shout.
How could you do this?
Why did you do this?
We can't wrap our minds around this.
This can't be real.
This can't be true.
The quick decision you made to kill yourself.
This, your mother tries to live with.
This your brothers, your sister, your children can't forget.
You did not know how so many hearts would break.
The love they wanted you to feel, to keep you here.
This had to have been a brief moment of insanity.
We all will try our best to live with this sadness. Without you.

WE WISH YOU WERE STILL HERE WITH US
Nonfiction

We sang at your funeral.
We said prayers.
We put up your pictures, so we could feel you there.
We let balloons go.
We have broken hearts.
We will never have any lasting answers.
We will never know why, you took your life.
We will have difficulty going on living for a while.
We loved you.
We all wish our love had been enough to save you.
We did not know you needed help.
We did not see any internal or outward struggle.
We did not think this could happen to someone so young.
We are left with sadness to carry.
We are left with the burden of guilt.
We are left with the pain of what more could have been done to prevent this. We wish you were still with us.

It melts my grey and I can see your face
My soul's sanity bleeds in colors

MARTHA BIRD

FROM MICHIGAN TO MINNESOTA...
AND NOW WRITING BACK TO MICHIGAN
Nonfiction

I am Nobody and I am Somebody. You don't know me but I remember you. You were there at the beginning for me. The beginning of my connection to Basketry.

It is 2017 and Minnesota has been my beloved home for the past 22 years. I am an artist. I am a weaver. I am a basket weaver. I am an integrative nurse. All of this began in Michigan. I'm thinking back to 1993 when I moved to Michigan for a short but impactful two year period. I am remembering that my journey with basketry began one typical day that became noteworthy.

Let me back up...I was living in Massachusetts, working at a job I loved when I heard and felt a pop in my back, with subsequent pain down one of my legs. It happened at work and that was the end of my full time nursing career, just like that, in an instant. To make a long story short, I saw a lot of doctors, did a lot of treatments, and was put on modified bed rest. I could only go back and forth to the doctor and get up to do basic living tasks, otherwise I needed to be laying down to see if my back would heal. (The treatment is much different nowadays.) I followed the doctor's direction and "laid low" for two years. There was no improvement.

Having been raised in Wisconsin, I wanted to return to the Midwest. I landed in Grand Blanc, Michigan for a couple of years before heading over to Minnesota. While in Michigan, I decided the approach the doctor was recommending was not improving my back any. Furthermore, it was leaving me feeling isolated and depressed. It had been two years of bedrest and the end of a vital career. So I decided to get up and DO something.

I signed up for a class to learn how to make a basket. I don't remember what kind of basket I made or who the teacher was or even where exactly I took the class. All I know is I fell in love and dove in. I took class after class, joined a guild and went to the Association of Michigan

FROM MICHIGAN TO MINNESOTA... AND REACHING BACK AGAIN

Nonfiction

How do extraordinary things happen? By following the simple steps that lead there. In the last writing you learned about how my taking a basket weaving class, while living in Michigan, got me off bedrest. After initially immersing myself in my First Love of basket weaving, I moved on to exploring painting, mosaics, textiles, sculpture etc. I loved it all and emotionally and physically felt better when I was creating. As a nurse, I value the healing elements of expressing one's creativity and I decided I wanted to pursue that more fully.

Basketmaker's Convention in Grand Rapids in 1996. I bought cases of weavers' stain and coils of reed. I got a t-shirt, a bag, all my basket making tools. All of this happened in Michigan.

Fast forward to Minnesota...I joined the MN Basket Weaver's Guild, I took classes, and I worked in an art studio. Then I gave it up, even thought it was my First Love. Why? That is another story for another time. But I still identified as a Basket Weaver. I had my beloved baskets all over the house. People asked if I would sell them. I said no. I knew I wasn't making them anymore. I didn't want to let go of them.

Fast forward again...in 2015 I walked into another art studio space. My first thought was "ahhh, I could make baskets here." It was a guilty pleasure; I didn't tell anyone. I was working in other mediums at that time.

Fast forward again...in 2016 I joined an artist collective—again another story for another time. My being asked to join revolved around my basketry.

Today (2017) I have a dozen basket commissions I'm working on; I am curating and participating in a show at the Minnesota Landscape Arboretum and am traveling to Ireland to study with four basket makers.

As I was creating my artist resume I was tracing back dates. When did I start basket weaving? What years exactly? I Googled the Association of Michigan Basketmakers and found a link to your beloved newsletter editor, Susan Lawrence. I wanted help in nailing down the dates of my beginning. She was just the right person.

And here I am writing an article for you the Michigan Basket Maker's Association. I am nobody. I am somebody.

I asleep while I shivered! The best and the worst The Rip Van Winkle Effect.

BENJAMIN REVIER

INSPIRING HEART

Fiction

You should always strive to do better. Inspire yourself to do what needs to be done but also see forward and walk forward in life. You should inspire yourself to learn and keep learning because the only time you should have stopped learning is when you take the very last breath. Be inspired for it. Excitement for life gives a little spice in your world, in your community. Get excited about who you are and what you stand for, because there is no one else like you. Be inspired in your heart and then your mind surely will follow in suit. Get excited for a living because if you don't, your heart will turn gray and your mind will be empty.

MIND'S INQUISITION

Fiction

My mind is frail steel. The frailty is in its own design. Draw all messy on blue prints. Collecting dust in the caverns of my own soul. The cavern lights have burnt out. As I explore the caverns of my mind, the wind drifts in and out. As I go further into the cavern, my feet get heavier and heavier. My feet feel like heavy lead weights. The pounding of my feet echoes through the caverns. As I search through somberness and emptiness, the isolation is the somberness of the cavern. The emptiness consumes. It eats up all hope. But there's a little whole mess in it. There is a little relief in the empty darkness.

YELLOW

Fiction

Yellow is the color of happiness. I'm not talking about materialism or self-importance or self-indulgence. I'm talking about a true yellow – not a whitewash yellow, not a yellow you can put on a shelf or put on his clothes. I'm talking about a yellow that's inside all of us and it shouldn't burn as bright inside of us for all to see. I'm talking about integrity, self-dignity, contentment and empathy. I believe in the yellow spectrum. Contentment is most important because being comfortable where you're at in the present moment is a true testament of being happy. Being okay where you're at and who you are is

blossoming into dazzling brilliance
Distrust and disconnection
Replaced by insight, passion and kindly affection
Always seeking friendship
The sun was down so many years
But now it shines so bright
The spring flowers in their finest attire
Like the young chick afraid to leave its nest
Finally escaping into heavenly bliss
Lost but now found.

RIPVANWINKLE EFFECT

Poetry

Sometimes we find out dreams in mysterious and unexpected ways!
Hidden somewhere within us is is undiscovered potential!
Lost years, so deep led to a certain transfiguration
Into a joyous being
In my midyears I found the power of the written word
The horrendous thoughts
The destructive torment suddenly was slipping away
This affliction of my moods and thoughts
The self-destructive demons
Not blending in with my fellow beings
Quickly changing to the excited creature
The bubbling beauty, overwhelming passion
Joining the crowds, craving company
Not just writing but unrelenting love of my fellow species
Kindly relations and affection
This peace so good, so welcome
This exuberant, energetic appetite for creativity, for living
Somehow born from the darkness
The fullness of life birthing my artistic talent
My passionate love of life bursting into exuberant creative art
Bringing refreshment to the eye
So uplifting to my moods
Up unto the heavens, so high, where the eagles soar
So free, so alive
The angelic beings' halos radiate
Their splendid brilliance
So fantastically dazzling
Extravagant travels and memories put in colorful beauty
For all to see
The withering moods no more

last fall, to join a collective of artists. This core group is supported by Avivo ArtWorks through studio space, art supplies, career counseling, and exhibition opportunities. It was after the second denial that I asked for feedback from the Program Coordinator as to why I was not chosen. She told me it would be helpful to show a dominant art form. We went back and forth me saying I didn't have one, her saying I did. Finally I asked, "Well then, what is it?" She said, "Your basketry!" I replied, "That's craft, not art." She said, "Who told you that?' It was an idea I had picked up over the years. She helped me understand that at the level I was working at; it could definitely be visual art. I've been grappling with how to make that transition. I applied for a couple of grants with that question at the heart: How do I transition from craft to art?

It was at this point that a fellow collective member expressed concern wondering if her very large piece of artwork would ever find a home with a buyer. It is a beautiful piece, so I thought of a contact I had at the MN Landscape Arboretum and was introduced to the curator. I learned that they only accept donated art, but in the process, the curator looked at the collective website and said she loved the work and was interested in doing a show with us. Furthermore, she looked at my Flickr portfolio, saw I was a basket maker and said that she would like to commission nine fishing creel baskets for the fish/water-themed show (MN is known as the Land of 10,000 Lakes). I told her I had never made a creel and that I would try one and if I could pull it off AND I enjoyed myself then I would accept the commission.

The show **Water's Edge** opened last year at the Minnesota Landscape Arboretum, the recently voted #1 Botanical Garden in the United States. I was given the honor of curating the show of 15 collective artists. All nine baskets were made as requested and were on display in the exhibit and gift shop. Several sold.

It has been a surprise and great honor to curate the show and share my baskets with the public. A year ago, I never would have imagined I would be in this place now. Big things can happen when you just one step at a time and follow the thread that is before you.

FROM MINNESOTA TO IRELAND...AND BACK AGAIN

Nonfiction

I've had my richest travel experiences when I have traveled the world alone, depending on the kindness of strangers to help me feel connected and a sense of belonging in the world. I ventured off on a trip to Ireland in June 2017 to enrich my understanding of a people and culture through 1:1 study with 4 basket makers. I'd be gone the month of June 2017, knowing it would change who I am and leave its mark on my expression as an artist.

The first day I drove on the opposite side of the street through the narrow, narrow lanes, humming to myself as I reached a tricky spot, knuckles white. When I arrived at the nearest city, tears fell down my cheeks as I was so happy to have arrived. As instructed, I tried to call and email my first teacher Paul to let him know he could come lead me the last leg of the way. I couldn't get either communication method to work so I walked into Fitzpatrick's and asked the woman behind the counter if she could help me by calling him for me. She dialed the phone and handed it to me. When I hung up, I told her what a big learning curve it was for me to drive on the left side of the street and that I was a bit flustered at not being able to contact Paul. She smiled at me and said, "Would you like a cone, dear?" I said, "What?" She said, "Would you like an ice cream cone?" I asked how much it would be and she said, "No, no just have a cone, dear." And I sat there, leaning against my car, puffy eyes from crying, licking probably the most delicious cone I'd ever had because of the kindness.

It adventure began with Paul, I would trust him to figure out ANYTHING— he is an amazingly talented artist and basket maker that has incredible skill in sculptural works. I wanted to create a sculptural basket. He taught me the beginnings and then we each went on to create our own version. He grappled briefly with how to end his; I watched and saw it was very, very complicated so went with ending mine in a simpler upside down creel-like fashion.

Barry was an incredibly talented teacher who really worked with me to understand the concepts of basketry. His goal for me wasn't to create a basket; it was to teach me as many techniques as he could, to incorporate into my own work once I got home. I did 5 bases with him just to cement how to make them tight and round. I got to walk through his beautiful willow garden of 75+ varieties and sleep in a private log cabin and soak in the hot tub at night. I was included as a member of the family with meals, conversations, hot tubbing and playing with the grandchildren. Well, also what might compete with that little girl hug was the first day I arrived in Dublin, jet lagged, exhausted but needing to stay awake to effectively make the time transition. I walked over to Gogarty's Temple Bar and sat down at the bar. There was an amazing guitarist and banjo player. At the break, I talked with the guitarist and when the last set started, I sat and listened as that old Irish man dedicated the song to "This woman, here all the way from Minnesota." How is it that the world shrinks down to the size small enough to have a song dedicated to you on first meeting in a new country? What an Irish welcome.

And then back to the kindnesses of Barry...I was so worn out from the challenges of driving—like when I started to go on to automatic pilot and noticed 2 headlights heading straight for me and realized I'd drifted over

In legend on its island home
Among the many beautiful birds are the brilliant cockatoos
Only here is the reptilian mammal, the rare platypus
A duck's bill, a beaver's tail, and lays eggs
All these fabled animals found here!

LOST AND FOUND
Poetry

This mysterious pain
Somewhere in my brain
The disease of the ages
The quiet desperation
My mind goes to dark places
Like the deepest dungeon
The withering terror
The ever lingering horror
Always treacherous chaos
The ever searching soul
Looking for peace and content
Instead of havoc
The wretched wreck
The fearful betrayal of my thoughts
Defies my ability to reason
Misled by my wild imagination
That takes me to unending torment
The grueling despair
The frailness of life
Alive but not living
Early on not destined for the
Same fate as others
Suspicion and suspense
Quiet seclusion
My own worst enemy
Haunted by past demons
Psychological deception
Lost in the disease of the brain
Suddenly like an exploding volcano
Unleashing fire
A thunderous array of brilliance
A burst of energetic uplifting spirits
I'm alive, free from the dire torment
Passion that knows no rival
Gregarious excitement

and a long day, drove in the opposite direction of his home to meet me and lead me through the streets so I didn't have to continue the mantra "Stay left, look right" for those last few minutes of the evening. And sitting at the kitchen table with me, helping me map out the directions for my stops, highlighting my whole huge map of Ireland for me–so I'd know where I'd been and where I was going. I appreciated him walking me through the directions so I'd feel the confidence to get to each place.

I signed up for a skib class with Ciaran that was supposed to last from 9:30 am - 5:30 pm. Fatigue was setting in so I didn't get to a stopping point until 7:15 pm when I wasn't even done with the basket yet. Even so, he showed me how to make a rattle that took me until 7:45 pm. He invited me back the next day to finish the border without further mention of more money or expression of frustration. When arriving the next morning, he was cheerful as ever and when I shared that I was very worried about how I was going to get the baskets back home, he arranged for me to meet with his father, Joe, so I could get my treasures home. When I completed my time with Ciaran, the ATM was out of service. He wanted to be sure I had enough cash to pay the next basket maker, so said, "Save your cash for that next basket maker and just pay me when you get back in a few days." His generosity was astounding.

And on to Vincent, the magnificent storyteller, life teacher and amazing lover of all things baskets. He lives on the Aran Islands and travels every year to teach basketry at the Milwaukee Irish Fest and has a loyal following there that buy out all his wares every year. He shared a story of a 98-year-old basket maker as well as taking basketry into the nursing home where an older gentleman simply twirled willow around a stick. Vincent, keeping the aides at bay that wanted to say he wasn't doing it right said, "He's happy and making a beautiful basket in his mind...so he is doing it exactly right." Vincent explains that he makes baskets for the sheer pleasure of it– sometimes 18 hours a day. "Make the basket for yourself and yourself alone. If you make it to hold a potato and it holds a potato, it's a perfect basket. The only important thing is that you are happy." He buoyed my confidence in myself as a basket maker. He said it doesn't matter how long it takes you to make a basket or what it looks like, if you are happy, that is it. There is no competition, there is no comparison. It is his love of the basket maker that warmed my heart especially, knowing I was in that category.

And finally, my inspiring afternoon at Joe's home was complete with brown bread and tea. The opportunity to talk with The Teacher who-teaches-the-teachers. Not ever having met me before, he kept my baskets in the sun for a week so they wouldn't mold, placed them in one of his

I need to be busy in life!
It keeps me on the straight and narrow.
Not on the big and broad way. Others can do that.
Like butterflies,
Fluttering from one flower to another.
I cannot stand being flighty!
Structure is key.
It keeps trouble at bay.
All work, and no play,
May make Jack a dull boy.
But I need to work on things.
It makes "Jill" happier.

GARY R. MELQUIST

CREATURES OF THE MOONLIGHT
Poetry

As the day's heat softens
And the sunshine drifts away
The Aussie Outback comes to life
The nocturnal creatures find safety
Under the moon's dim light
The Australian sunset
Hides nighttime's life
The wombat leaves its burrow
The ferry penguins return from the sea
Bringing food to their young chicks in their sand dune hideouts
The evening moon brings safety from
The birds of prey
The eucalyptus is both home and nourishment for the delightful koala
This marsupial unlike its cousins, the wombat
Or kangaroos, is found not down under but up high
This tree is protection and safety
For the outback's deadly serpents
Are always on the prowl
The deadly taipan has no rivals for its toxic venom
Creatures of fantasy glide from tree to tree These flying foxes found
nowhere but here The Tasmanian tiger is no more!
But this mysterious fellow still lives

post office. All after I had left. When I asked him why he would do this for me, a stranger, he said "The basket community is small. We have to do this kind of thing for each other."

The time in Ireland, enchanting. The beautiful feel and smell of willow edifying, the kindness of the people extraordinary. And the 4 very different, very wonderful experiences with basket makers has changed who I am. They have left their mark on me and I look forward to seeing how that is reflected in my artwork.

D.D.

7-10 SPLIT
Poetry

he swung the ball high and threw
it hard down the alley, his right leg
momentarily an arabesque and got a
7-10 split which he miraculously
picked up for a spare and I thought he
could walk on water

SHE DREAMED OF FISH
Poetry

She had dreamed of fish that became her fifth child, and her hand never
itched so she couldn't really afford another mouth that gulped like a
guppy on her engorged nipple while 1-4 sat and watched cartoons on a
flat screen TV that the middle child's father had bought her hot from the
man on the corner because his priorities were in the wrong place but he
had given his son his last name on the birth certificate. So there, she'd
told her naysayers. So there!

THEFT
Poetry

Virginia stood at the front of the bodega intent
on paying for her 25 cent bag of dipsy doodles
and her 2 for $1.00 off-brand soda when a
ragamuffin in torn blue jeans and a dirty midriff
halter top walked up to the counter, too.

Then amplify your voice with Michelle Obama's who grew up in the 90s area out the Chicago L. Relate John Dos Passos' varied journalist styles to the powerful voice Michelle Obama has given to women and America as the first wife of a president to graduate from an Ivy League University, Princeton. Build your voice against Michelle Obama's and amplify these stories in 2018, a history bracketing year with purpose and practice.

STEVE PECK

CHANGES
Poetry

Change can be as sudden as a surprise.
Change can be as subtle as a feather in the wind.
Change can be as profound as the turning of the seasons.
Change can be as small as turning the page in a book.
Change can be big, like a wedding event.
Change can be minute, as a tiny cell dividing through mitosis.
Change can be done by a few.
Change can result just from me.
Change is always imminent somewhere.

IN A NUTSHELL
Poetry

My life has been interesting.
I have seen it all.
Fights, abuse, restraints.
Nothing surprises me anymore.
I also have experienced it.
All of the above!
In a nutshell.
The MMPI is like my life story.
The Rorschach Test, my coloring book.
My life seems a best-selling novel.
Moving out of state was my personal Vietnam.
My first fiancée left me alone.
In a nutshell.
But, I am alive.
I am surviving.
I have conquered a lot.
Life is getting better. I am not finished yet. In a nutshell...

this day she wasn't sure whether she was complicit or a victim but she watched as if s ogging through mud, went outside herself and saw herself place a $20.00 bill on the filthy, torn green velvet counter top. The Arab behind the counter didn't grab the currency fast enough and the ragamuffin snatched the twenty and ran out the door. Virginia never even reached out to touch her but turned a blind eye to the theft. Ragamuffins require money more than the poor and even though it was Virginia's last, she let the thief join her parents who sold bottled water and peeled oranges and sliced pineapples while walking up and down the middle of traffic before the exit onto the Henry Hudson Parkway. There are no takers, no one buys.

MARIA DAVIS

REFRESHED
Poetry

I feel new when I can wake up to a new day.
I feel new when I can feel the warm breeze brushing my cheek as it runs through my hair.
I feel new when I see dogs playing with their silly quirks
I feel new when I see butterflies pollinate on my favorite flowers
To be new is not impossible when you clear your mind and relax by draining the negative energy out of your body
To be new is possible when you are true to yourself.

IF I COULD TALK TO ANIMALS
Nonfiction

If I were able to talk to animals I would thank God for this amazing gift. I would tell the birds to keep singing and talking, it is very soothing to me. I would tell the bees, your sting bites, but keep pollenating—we need the honey.

I would apologize to the frogs and toads for kissing them, but I can't help it! They're too cute. Your croaking during mating season is music to my ears.

---

of ... , ... , ... and the interim period reflect the complexity paradigm. Algebra has four principles, the associative, the distributive, the commutative and the inverse. These laws and paradigm reflect in a new law complexity due to individual variation.

Al Nier, a Regents physics professor at the University of Minnesota, founded the field of biomass spectroscopy. Plotting, planting, and plotting plodding theory of the universe.
4 trees! Freud's categories verses Aristotle's come into play.

Neuroimaging is an evolutionary offshoot of biomass spectroscopy.

I HEAR CHICAGO SINGING
Poetry

I Hear Chicago Singing.
I hear the cool songs of Chicago Blues in the voices of the student leaders.
The coarse, rough song voices reverberate in the bus drivers on the 3 off the L.
The woman book kiosk seller chants as she markets her medium.
The Asian Today newscasters is a Blythe spirit as she sings the pain of the youth lost in a cave off China's Coast.
Sing with the delicate singing and cooing of the Chicago daycare mothers at the Socialism8 conference.
Chant, "Fight is possible. We are unstoppable. Another world is possible."

JOHN DOS PASSOS, CHICAGO MENTOR, THE TRIBUTE, THE STORY
Fiction

John Dos Passos, Chicago author, mentor, invites you to The Larger Narrative Invitation in history literature and art.

John Dos Passos stands in literature against the sentimental, self-defensive and partial and ethnic and often easy to dismiss authors. His odd narratives and stories have an unusual trance quality about them that many authors lack. His work is a mural of American figures.

John Dos Passos Reference Library is an Odyssey.
USA Trilogy, 42nd Street, 1919, the Big Money, Travel Books, Manhattan Transfer, Three Soldiers, the Best Times: An Informal Narrative; One Man's Initiative 1917; the 14th Chronicle; Orient Express;

Connect your story to the Larger Narratives and Landscapes.

I would tell the dogs, all of them are adorable and special in their own way. I love the fact that they're so loyal and forgiving no matter what they've been through.

I would also tell them that I like them a lot, better than some humans. Their silly quirks I find humorous and make me laugh. Whenever I see y'all out with your human family I want to pet you and say hello. I am blessed to have you in my life. My dogs have seemed to understand my moods and have done so many therapeutic things for me. I am eternally grateful.

LIFELINE
Nonfiction

As I investigate this never-ending hole in the earth's crust I try to remember how I got here. I recall the vivid paralyzing flash backs, bad memories, and nightmares that got me on this path and I start to feel the ground trembling beneath me. The sound I hear is like no other sound I've heard before. It sounds like an avalanche combined with an earth quake or like two dominating animals fighting for the alpha role in the kingdom. Suddenly, I feel the dirt and rocks slipping from underneath me. I feel so unstable as I begin to fall into this unknown abyss. I begin to feel and hear my heart beat, like a drummer doing a solo at a rock concert.

The further down I go I begin to smell a raunchy odor, which smells like a decaying body and rotten eggs. I am so scared that the walls in this hole are closing in on me. Help! Help! Help! I say in a low and raspy voice. Can anyone hear me? I'm thinking that my cries are falling on closed ears. Should I try to conserve my energy by not shouting? As I try to figure out how to solve the puzzle of life, I hear a faint voice in the distance, which is one I didn't recognize. The voice sounds so soothing and nurturing, like when loving parents talk to their child. I can't quite hear or understand what they're saying.

The voice is getting louder, however not overbearing. I finally realize that the voice is calling my name. The beaming voice shouts: I'm going to throw you a life line. The confident voice gives me specific instructions on how to get into the harness and starts to lift me up while telling me to hang on tight and not let go.

On the way up, I begin to feel the cold air evaporating like condensation on an ice-cold beverage outside in the middle of summer. I notice the raunchy odor starting to dissipate like a tornado disappearing after it creates so much havoc. The kind voice keeps reassuring me that I'm fine and everything is okay.

I am from the maple steeling from Boston, setting on a plant to Minnesota, stretching its legs into nothing but a wet paper towel.

I am from goulash and Tupperware, from Donna and Kent.
I'm from "he's teasing me!" and "you crybaby!" from "clean up this room right now,"
and "you all better behave or else."
I'm from my cup runneth over,
and two stick and yarn God's eyes.

I am from Ness and Larson: from potlucks in the church basement, and from tuna casseroles in Corningware.
I am from surely goodness and mercy
and a cardboard church filled with pennies.

I am from Kingsbury and Barclay, from fried fish and crazy cake.
From the fishing with Grandpa for walleyes, and when we cleaned fish, from the rocks he showed us were behind the sheepshead's eyes.

I am from these moments—fed to the maple tree from Boston, taller now than us all.
It rises like a flame in autumn among the nineteen oak trees, legs planted deep, arms stretched wide open, ready to receive.

Nonfiction

DR. PATRICK O'DOUGHERTY
A TRIBUTE TO AL NIER, PHYSICS PROFESSOR AND FOUNDER OF THE FIELD OF BIOMASS SPECTROSCOPY, WHICH REVOLUTIONIZED THE MEDICAL FIELD

Al Nier biomass spectroscopy Founder, throwing bouquets at stars!

Reinventing Physics: the Dialectical Debate in Physics!
The most fertile area in the medical field in recent years is the mapping areas.

Story: Al Nier invited Patrick O'Dougherty to his office in the Physics building to brown bag a lunch and discuss the Dialectical Debate in Physics with him. He told me the tale of how Nils Bohr left his galoshes or rubbers when Nils Bohr gave a lecture at the physics department. Patrick O'Dougherty argues Thesis, antithesis, synthesis resolve in complexity. The Marxist and Fuerbach paradigm is too easy.

(I had finally got all the charcoal out of them) and the next day she snuck scissors into the hospital in her purse, and in between fifteen minute checks gave me a haircut. "There," she said, satisfied, slipping the scissors back into her purse. She took the hair clippings too, so we wouldn't be found out. I don't know if the hospital staff ever noticed, but if they did, they didn't say anything.

Even now, when I write the word "hospital," still I hesitate—for the Erich Lindemann Mental Health Center was, to me, not a hospital but an institution with sickly pale green walls and an unnatural quietness that pervaded throughout, interrupted only by occasional outbursts from the patients, or soft conversations between the staff.

Footsteps echoed down the hallways, pausing before each door. I learned to distinguish between the short, brisk step of the nurse and the sliding, slow-motioned gait of the patient that followed her in flip-flop slippers, imitating her going on her rounds. The man startled me the first time he looked in my room. He had an odd expression on his face and I didn't know what he was going to do. He looked at each of us—my mom, Tammy, and I—then left, closing the door so slowly behind him that I watched it, waiting for that click that made me feel at least somewhat secure.

The staff wrote down in my file that I was afraid of the other patients. It wasn't, however, fear of the patients so much as the fear, deep down, that perhaps I really was like them. What if there was some kind of mistake, and I was forced to stay here?

On the last night I once more slept under the ceiling without stars. The next day I would be on an airplane to Minnesota, and then straight to another hospital's locked psychiatric unit from the airport. Those were the conditions of my release. So focused was I on getting out, I neglected to account for the same item most people do when running away: your problems come with you. My depression, my looming darkness, would follow me no matter where I was. I needed to confront it, for it's what landed me in the hospital in the first place. What lay in front of me was an uncharted destination. I had no map to guide me, and definitely no stars.

FAMILY TREE
Poetry

I am from the grandfather clock at the top of the stairs, from Kenmore and Sears.
I am from the acorns that drop down each fall from nineteen oak trees.

The Power Tower ride at Valley Fair. I can now see the faint sunlight reappearing out of the hole, which is reassuring me that I am almost out of the hole. The voice encourages me that I am doing good and that we're almost out of the hole.

I finally see the opening of the hole get bigger and bigger. I am amazed at what I see next the rays of the sun coming through the clouds. I am finally out of the hole. I am so happy and thankful for the help, I begin to cry and repeatedly thank the voice. The voice tells me, "This is what I am here for. I will catch you whenever you fall no matter what happens. All I ask is that you keep believing in me and never lose your faith."

I am finally at peace.

LINDA DYER

HAPPINESS IS RED
Poetry

Happiness is red
It sounds like wind blowing quietly
It tastes like coffee with hot chocolate and ice cream
It smells like root beer candy
Happiness feels like getting into a warm blanket on a cold winter morning.

IN MY RIVER
Poetry

In my river, I am a catfish because I like my whiskers and my bubble eyes.
I am in the Mississippi and can go and go with the other fish.
In my river, I see a fishing hook but swim around it. I never get caught.
In my river, I see many other fish who are my friends.
You are a rainbow fish. You are my friend.

PARTY IN THE PARK
Nonfiction

One time there were some kids playing at a park and I sat down to watch them play. They were having fun, having a tea party with their dolls, using water for the tea and sitting on a blanket. Then they went and played in the swing with their dolls and the see-saw. I was watching them for about an hour and then they went home and I went home too. I had a good time, thinking of when I was a little girl.

MAMA ETHEL

I AM OLD AND NEW

Poetry

I feel old when I can't get out of bed
I feel new when I can walk without a cane
I feel old when my problems begin to bother me
I feel new when I dream sweet dreams
I feel old when my children think they are smarter than me. I feel new when I know that it's not true
To be new is impossible when I let these things get to me
To be new is possible when I don't let these things get to me

THE LESSONS OF COURAGE AND FEAR

Poetry

In my life I've known Courage.
We met when I was thirteen, learning to swim and almost drowned.
Nowadays Courage comforts me when I am scared.
I find Courage when I am determined to do things I want to do.

In my life I've known Fear. We met when I went under the water and couldn't get up.
These days Fear is creeping up behind me when I'm in a position I think I can't get out of. Fear finds me when I'm in a position I can't get out of.

I've learned that Courage and Fear are different—
When Courage tells me to try to do something I will do my best. Fear says, "You can't do it," but really I can.

Usually I listen to my gut.
I wish my Courage would stay with me forever. I wish Fear would leave me forever.

Fear makes me angry when I see so much hate and no love in this world I wish I had the Courage to show people how much love there is in this world to make the world change because if we brought love and joy to each other there wouldn't be so much depression and stress in our lives.

climb out the window. I might buy some more time by using the old pillow trick, the one where you stuff pillows under the blanket to make it look like someone is sleeping there. It was so obvious it just might work. But the window of course, would never open. Breaking it would be out of the question, for the noise.

Once again, all options had closed in on me; even the ones I imagined proved impossible. I wanted to disappear, and so going back to the bed from the window without a view, I climbed up near the head and sat on the pillow, holding my knees close to my chest, retreating into my shell. From the door it would look like I was not there because a closet blocked the view of the head of the bed. If only it were true.

When the nurse came by on her rounds she did not see me from the doorway. She walked into the room, and when I looked up the flashlight was in my face and I couldn't see. She moved the light to the side, out of my eyes and asked if I was all right. "No!" I answered, crying, and she asked me if I wanted to talk. I shook my head. She asked if I wanted her to get my doctor.

"No. Just leave me alone."

"Do you want me to give you something to help you sleep?"

That's all I need, for them to drug me, I thought. I'm not taking any pills they give me. I don't need her. I don't need anybody.

*****

I spent my days in my room, leaving only to go to the bathroom or get my meal tray. Perhaps it was because I was only there on a seventy-two hour hold that they extended privileges to me that were not given to the other patients; I could eat in my room, have longer visiting hours—the other patients could not. The first time I took my tray, a woman pointed at me and said, "You have to eat in here with us. You can't eat in your room." I told her the staff told me I could and then I left the room, carrying my tray with me. I didn't want to make an issue of it. I didn't want the other patients to know I was getting special treatment. But I could feel the woman's eyes on me as I walked to my room.

I cannot remember days being so long. I tried to sleep them off. Waking was the worst. When I woke I saw the walls around me and remembered.

My mother and my roommate, Tammy, came to visit each morning at 9:00 AM. Our conversations were interrupted every quarter hour by the

Kelly - We are all at the table without you and it hurts to not have you there. Pat and now Janice, Sharon and Bryce and Randy, and Dad and Mary and me alone as I have always been.

You were a bridge to pull us all together and a tornado to tear us apart. Mom never sat at the table with all of us as adults but you did.

And now you are gone. And mom is gone and Bryce is an adult and Pat and I are now in our 60s and we held a funeral for you 2 years ago. Without you, the magic has gone out of FL, where I had so much fun with you. The alligators we saw on walks and in the water are no longer strong and dangerous but have turned into small, cheap gift shop souvenirs. The toucans, pelicans and great blue herons have all flown away. And a strong, cold wind continues to blow from the ocean onto the shore.

And now there is a place on the Cemetery's memorial wall with your name on it.

And I still miss you.

JILL LYNNE NESS

A NIGHT WITHOUT STARS
Nonfiction

Night came again, and I lay in bed, trying to make myself believe that I was in my own apartment, beneath the quilts, looking up at the ceiling filled with (some would say childish) glow in the dark star decals. Before I ever moved in, I had planned to put them up there, because I never could at home. But the first night at the apartment I shut off the lights and found the stars already there, placed by some tenant before me. In time I acquired more stars, and planets, and at night slept under a whole universe.

But here at a state hospital in Massachusetts, involuntarily committed due to a suicide attempt, the ceiling of my room had no stars. When I walked to the window to look outside for real stars, they couldn't be seen either, because of the city's lights and smog. I didn't know how long the building had been around, but it did not escape my attention that in the not-too-distant past, a place such as this would not be called a "Mental Health Center," but an "Asylum" or "Hospital for the Insane."

Every fifteen minutes the nurses came by my room on their checks. I knew that even if I wanted to, there wouldn't be enough time to escape, either by reality or by death. They'd find me out either way. If I found a way to

---

...taking in themselves, Love is free— it doesn't take money to give it, it doesn't take money to take it— and that is all the Courage we need, because God is love. We should never have to Fear for anything.

WORDS HURT
Nonfiction

I don't like you telling me what to do. You don't know how I feel when you criticize the things I do. You make me feel like a wilting flower.

You don't know how I feel when you assume to know what I did when you are not around or otherwise disrespect my feelings. Getting into other peoples' business is not pretty. You never respect my feelings or you would never do these things. We really need to close our mouths and be quiet. You never show the love and kindness we so deserve.

We should "stop." We never admire peoples' talent for what they do. All we need is a kind word we deserve to make us feel special. To give it doesn't cost a thing.

I live day to day trying to show love and getting nothing in return. I live everyday listening to people talking to each other without feeling for each other. How can people be so cold-hearted? It makes me feel mad and sad.

You don't know how I feel. I see people not caring about the next person in pain. Your feeling of pain is no harder than anyone's. We live in pain every day. Why can't we love each other the way God loves us? The agape love, not criticizing each other, letting people do their thing.

"Who are you?" Stop telling me what to do. It's not your business to say a thing. It depresses me and stresses me out so stop telling me what to do. Words hurt.

AMBER FISHER

GRANDMA
Poetry

She is portals of prayer at 6am
She is thinned coffee

spelling things like beautiful or refreshing. She is full of roots in jars and budding maples.

She's an old Jack-in-the-box when she's mad.
When she's happy, she is a light-hearted flowering crab apple blossom.
She sounds like a ceramic bird making sweet songbird calls.
She looks like a sunrise, multiple colors rising in her eyelids.

ECHO G. MITCHELL

SUICIDE DRAGON
Poetry

Two years eight months after the death of my protector-August 1992)
Unguarded, unprepared, unaware, I stroll into a day.
Memory bubbles up images of a baby; shining eyes, laughing mouth.
My lips curl in replication, emit a throaty gurgle such as
I had heard from that small person long ago in another place.
Suddenly, tears gather in the corners of my eyes, whisper, "It's all right.
That was then, my baby, when our souls were so close. I miss you, but...
You know... I wish you happiness now."
Wandering from room to room, I pass a certain closet door.
The suicide dragon jumps out, relentlessly wraps his claws around my throat, cutting off my breath.
I can't escape him! He subjugates my will.
A strangled cry squeaks past my lips, "Help me!" No one answers...no one hears.
Fear and anguish fuel my attempt to reach release.
Stumbling into the kitchen, I fumble for my friends: bottles with numbers, containing relief.
"Please," I beg, "Please work for me this time."
Spontaneously, I chant an ingrained lyric,
"God, I can't do this again. God, I'm so tired.
Do you understand? God, just let me see you.
Please take this black dragon off my neck." The image of that grown-up baby appears before my eyes.
"Yes, God, I know this vision has worked before.
But...I can't Please believe me, I can't do it anymore." A rationalization-apology counters this connection with the world.
"My baby please forgive me, though it might take you some time. Just believe I did my best for you, even with this sick mind." The dragon rakes his claws again, deeper, into my brain.
In agony, in clumsy haste, I shake out all the pills.

I look upon these feet that walk upon these streets
And I know I will always remember the street
And reminisce on how far I came

Even trudging along these crooked sidewalks
All along the cracked concrete
And graffiti etched under the bridges
That strangely comfort me
The street holds so many secrets
For the street never speaks
And I am comforted by the strangers
I will never see again
But the street silently acknowledges and conceals each story
Which is written within its rich history
A story for the ages
But the street cannot speak

MICHELE

IT'S HOT TODAY IN FLORIDA
Poetry

Its hot today. Kelly and I remember when I visited you one June in FL
and it was very hot. On the water it was OK and in the grass and in the
shade, it was pretty comfortable but hotter than hell in the parking lot at
Home Depot. We'd run there you see to get a new light fixture for your
bathroom. I remember that your car was nice and cool - you had great AC.
We stepped out of the car into the parking lot and it didn't seem that bad.
Into the store we went. We weren't there that long - just long enough
to grab the light fixture and pay for it. Out we came. The black asphalt
pavement now radiated heat. You opened your car door and heat boiled
out. The car was now a roasty, toasty 250 degrees I think. You calmly
climbed into the car and turned on your AC while I stood outside trying
to decide which way I would rather die - from being roasted or boiled
Thankfully the car cooled down in a few minutes and away we went. But
for a few short minutes it was like roasting in hell. And now that you have
left this life, I think of you and our trip to Home Depot whenever it is go
degrees outside and boiling hot.

Poetry

The street it echoes
All the unique lives that pass
The footsteps cracked concrete
Of lives led of every conceivable perspective

The street is bouncing with life
And every face is etched in its history
As I stroll by
I breathe in everything
That is-the street

The footsteps reverberate
As if echoing a beautiful symphony
And it is a mystery the direction each step will take
The street is always happy you came
And it never judges
For it is merely a street
It will give you company
On your way back home
Into the unknown

There are distracting sights to see
Sometimes celebrations and laughter
Sometimes upon these streets, tragedy
But what keeps me coming back
Are the people

Stepping upon cracked concrete
Moving in every direction life might take them
At times the light shines bright
Hastening into a diner with friends
Or the sign that says open late
Drinks shared and cares eased away

To all the feet that have walked this street
And the secrets the street will keep
Under the street light
I could go anywhere
Within these sidewalks
Left disarray

As darkness descends around my head, I whimper,
"Oh God, please let me into the light."
I wake sometime after, with tubes descending my throat.
Doctors and nurses; concerned, some just looking tired, discuss my condition as if I weren't there.

Later, numbly walking in lock-ward halls,
I wonder what new drug they'll try this time. For weeks following my return home,
I superstitiously watch the closed closet door.
I'm feeling stronger. But, when the perilous full moon glows in the dark cloudless sky, I avert my eyes.
The trembling returns when I pass that fearful door.
The insidious dragon is waiting, sheltered in the dark.
Meanwhile I keep praying for protection, searching for more light.

(10 years 8 months after the death of my protector March 2003)

I believe I am finally rid of that dragon. He hasn't been lurking in my closet for some time now. I suppose he has found residence in the closet of someone else more vulnerable than I am. Thank you God for my relief, and I pray for the light to penetrate for whomever the dragon is lurking now.

Written while continuing to find remedies for my Bi-Polar condition and relief from my seizures. I found a woman who did EEGNEURO Biofeedback. I spent five years going to weekly therapy sessions. My epilepsy seizures stopped and my suicidal depressions finally relented. My Bi-Polar mood swings moderated and people told me I appeared to be a new person.

I was, in fact, since I had received a miracle healing for my brain. The claim of it being a miracle is true. In December I had lain on my carpet with tears, snot running all over, unable to pray or know how I would survive. I could only say: "God. Mercy." It was a week later that I found this therapist. I also realized that all my previous suicidal efforts did not succeed because God was not ready for me to be in the next Realm. He kept pushing me back. I believe I could almost hear God saying, "You are not done with your assignment!" But that is a different story.

THE FLOW OF ENERGY IN THE PHILLIPS-WANGENSTEEN BUILDING
Fiction

Amidst the soft babble of partial sentences, punctuated by abrupt greetings and farewells, the energy of anxiety and control mixes with honed-in concentration. Directed, then dispersed, the flow of energy is carried upward in the elevators, professionally deposited in small spaces accompanied by electrical, mechanical, organic assistance. The energy is harbored, delegated, relegated, conserved, and dispersed over the pre-planned apportioned time slots.

The flow of energy carried upward and downward in the elevators of the Phillips-Wangensteen building brings attendant wafts of anguish or relief. Positive and negative energy is enhanced by bestowed knowledge of the truth. Restrained terror is wrapped in hope of benign outcomes.

The Lords of Specialties carry clutches of evidence of their power to dispel or dispense despair. Their bland banter envelopes mortal, fatal, and mundane news. Thus they carry themselves in pseudo immortal clothing.

Perhaps, in the short run, this power provides nurturance for the expansion of ego. Perhaps in the middle run it gives grounds for intellectual and emotional growth. We can only hope that in the long run this experience of analysis of human woe, however specifically centered, can lead to an expansion of spiritual capacity and the ability to see each afflicted fellow human as a carrier of a soul, similarly as themselves, aimed towards connection with God.

Note: Written in fifteen minutes while waiting to find out if I might need brain surgery to correct a balance problem, vertigo. That kept me unable to walk for many episodes of hours or days.

LOQUASIOCITY: TALKING LIKE HRABAL
Fiction

The first thing is that I know that the word is not spelled right, but I decided some time ago that I wouldn't let my made up words be rejected just because they hadn't been discovered in the dictionary and I have been using this word for many decades to describe my problem, which is that I can't shut up even when I am alone you see and I keep talking in my head or out loud or whatever and people notice, especially when I am talking out loud they tend to look at me with this expression you know

TIFFANY LUECKEN

FLY OF THE EARTH
Poetry

Feeling smaller than a fly.
Maybe I'll just die.
To say I don't care what they believe is a lie.
Losing those you love is soaping up with lye.
The toxic waste fills you inside.
"Be strong" is a cliche, they say, when the wind could blow you.
Your significance fills up a thimble.
Why won't you self-combust?
Even those who chose you, have walked away. What is left, oh God?

MASK OH ME
Poetry

Oh mask what secrets do you hold?
Beautiful serene butterflies and roses emulate externally.
The person down the street believes I'm happy-go-lucky.
Truth lies somewhere inside.
Flames of anger and loss are not table talk.
Even friends grow pale when your life is a cloud raining blue tears and black dots.
Stay hidden my façade whispers.
Put the mask on.
No one will stay, look past the edges and find the beauty of you.

MOON WE SEE
Poetry

Giving up is no option.
I will swim across the ocean till my legs give out.
When my body tires, my spirit will guide me thru the wind.
The storms may pour yet I will hold tight to my conviction.
I will not stray from my path, which will lead me back to you.
James Horner et al (1986), American Tail, "peer out at the moon and know my love, I am thinking of you tonight."

and straps to put them in a four-point restraint. With grins on their faces, they back the person into a corner and tackle them. Having been through this experience, I am well aware of what drives a person to this point.

I will let the person rest and acclimate themselves to this sterile and antiseptic environment where opinions, emotions and rants are not tolerated. Nurses sit at their desks writing their deluded version of the story. I will the truth from the "horse's mouth," got groups and more groups.

Then a knight in shining armor appears under the spirituality—the clergy for the hospital with two degrees, one in divinity. He wants us to meditate, meditate, meditate. I want to know what he knows, but he puts up an incredible, impenetrable veil.

I'm out on the street again, no one to shoot me full of anti-psychotics, raid my room or shut the phone off...but I still wonder, what was behind that veil?

RUTH LAIS
PAINTER
Poetry

Self-doubt, anxiety, my mind it does race.
Institutions, medications, it's a cumbersome pace. Counseling, advice, wisdom and inspiration, it's hard to remember when you've lost all concentration. On social media, polarizing memes light up the screen.

No matter how I read them I'm not sure what they all mean.
But I know of a world where all stress subsides. Please dust off your feet and come on inside:

Linen or cotton - stretched or loose.
Crimson, ochre, cobalt, chartreuse.
Watercolor, acrylic, oil or gouache.
Wide, flat or round two inch paintbrush.
Abstract or still life, portrait, landscape.
Paint-laden brush stroke or pallet knife scrape.
Shapes, colors, shadows these forms they do take.
A playground before me, now what shall I make?

with this oh God don't you know when to shut up and I wouldn't really answer that question because I was usually in the middle of a sentence but my sentences tend to be very long so the middle is hard to find in fact periods are hard to find which would indicate that I don't understand English punctuation but that isn't right either I really do understand it I choose not to use it which is my right as an American citizen right? See, I do use some punctuation. There I proved it that I can be disciplined when I want to be but I was telling about this problem that has been with me my whole life apparently because my family have informed me that ever since I learned to put two words together I have not shut up and I found out that some of them were really annoyed if they got trapped in an elevator with me or in a room like a bathroom but my uncles loved it and I was never trapped in a bathroom with them thank God But I was telling you about my problem you see I have this thing with my brain that it won't shut down even when I am trying to sleep which is an example right now because I lay awake for five hours last night trying to sleep after working on my writing for twelve hours and my brain kept coming up with new ideas and I would have to get up turn on the light and put on my glasses and write down what was coming through my mind at that moment so I wouldn't lose it altogether because if I think of things while I am in bed and trying to sleep and I say no to my brain it just keeps on working anyway so I might as well get up and do something useful like saving the ideas so I can work out a solution to whatever has been going through my mind to keep me awake I am tired but as you see my brain won't shut up so I am then pretending to write but we all know that this is not a proper story But getting back to explaining this problem with my brain it is not apparently hereditary since no one else in my family has this phenomenon and some of them are entertained and will actually listen to me for several minutes or hours depending on their mobility and I have found that now that I am living in a Senior building and being happy here I have to be careful when I am using the elevator because some of these people give me that look I am so familiar with from my early days with my girl cousins and the girls at school well really some of the boys too which is the case now since many of the men not just the women look at me as if I am from Mars which is ridiculous since there is no atmosphere on Mars and no one could live there because it is also too cold for humans, with or without space suits But the only person I know of who might have this problem is the Hungarian writer Hrabal who made me happy and I laughed a lot when I read his book "Total Fear" which didn't seem to be about fear but about his mental conversations with an old girlfriend or lover or something but his writing is like my talking and now I am also writing like him although I am not copying him since I never had a girlfriend or even a lover It is just this tremendous freedom I am experiencing in writing like my brain is talking for once instead of forcing myself to use all those English language requirements that are so specific like the difference between lay and lie as if it matters as long as people know what you are saying don't you agree? Anyway this problem has gotten me in trouble on numerous occasions beginning with my girl cousins and progressing to almost every teacher I ever had all the way from kindergarten to a master's degree in college You might be surprised at this but my I.Q. is strange since it averages out to 115, but that is not helpful in understanding because the range is from 65 to168, or from 68 to 165, I forget but you get the picture if someone asked me what is your I.Q. I would have to say that is somewhere on a range between 65 and 168 depending on what particular area of the brain is being used at that moment if it was to balance my checkbook you would be sure to know that it is the low side of this mental equation that is being used but if it is to respond to the question what does this word mean I can go on for hours. Oh you have to go too bad but I understand and maybe I will see you again this is your floor and mine is two floors up. Have a good day!

Note: As indicated I wrote this after reading the Hungarian writer Bohumil Hrabal. His book: "Total Fear" is hilarious. I must have been in a depression when I read it because on page 162 I drew a smiley face with the note: "I can't die yet because I have to finish reading this book." Despite the lack of punctuation you might understand it as a one sided conversation in an elevator during a short ride.

SANDRA LYNN GEER

KEEP THY HEART
Nonfiction

God created us with our heart formed firstly, even before our brain starts being formed. The Heart is where compassion, charity, love, non-judgement, courage, patience, forgiveness, appreciation, gratitude and care live.

The heart is not just a ten ounce muscle that pumps blood and maintains circulation. The heart has its own independent nervous system. The heart transmits nerve impulses. It has hormones and neurotransmitters and pressure waves. There are at least several thousand neurons in the heart. Nerve cells that are found in various subcortical centers of the brain. Keep thy heart with all diligence; for out of it are the issues of life.

The heart is seen as a connection between the mind and body, forming a bridge between the two.

Because of the ever-growing scientific research on heart intelligence it may be time we develop a new personal attitude about following our hearts.

Linda has a trundle bed, I have a mattress on the floor. How can I live in such chaos—cake walk compared to the house I grew up in Fridley with two alcoholic parents, three brothers, over 150 reports for domestic abuse. But that's another story, maybe in next year's Artability. Sherry Dresner testified I have sixteen personalities; I estimate it to be way more than that but that's another story.

Seems I'm handed from one abusive situation to another. Being an expert escape artist I seek refuge at Bridgeview, the Law Library, the courthouse (armed sheriffs, video cameras) and various biker bars (another story). When it gets to be too much and I complain too much, I am committed (I believe five times). Bruises, not getting my medication and having to go through withdrawal, car accidents, pneumonia, pedophiles, Dr. Gilbertson, abortions, police, The Hell's Angels, people insulting me about the way I look, death threats, my phone and computer under surveillance (the court order is down at the court house), are all filed neatly under the heading:

PARANOID SCHIZOPHRENIA.

P.S. Who the hell is A.K.A. Linda Hoover really?

THE FRYING PAN
Poetry

I triple dog dare for you
to openly share your trip down the path
where we invite wrath
out of the pit we did get
out of the frying pan
into the fire we fan with
desire so hot we cannot
get out

UNITY HOSPITAL PSYCH WARD
Nonfiction

I am sitting in the Unity Hospital psych ward listening to KQRS 92.5 FM radio station, when they call a code green. All hell breaks loose when another person has arrived.

Vietnam vet with post-traumatic stress disorder, a domestic abuse with a black eye, a racial hate crime victim with a broken arm, a survivor of sexual abuse from a dominating religion...

Nonfiction

Garbage is piled up in the kitchen. The carpet is filthy; the bottoms of my feet are black from walking on it. Dirty diapers are filing the garbage can in the bathroom; the smell is nauseating. I can hear A.K.A. Linda Hoover's dog yelping in pain in her bedroom. God only knows what she is doing to her. The dog has gnawed at her paws, her nipples and her anus until they are raw. She is losing weight. I call the Humane Society, explain the situation. They tell me to call the police—I can't; I've had too many police calls—the staff will not give me my medication, the residents are stealing my belongings, and so on and so on. My social worker says if I keep calling the police I will be evicted. I walked over to the Holiday gas station to get a cup of coffee and two squad cars pulled me over.

Feces are stuck to the bottom of the toilet. I buy Comet and a brush at the dollar store to clean up the mess. Linda claims to be allergic to Comet. Battle after battle after battle. Her brand new flat screen TV blasts away 24/7. There is free Wi-Fi but I don't receive a signal. Linda does in her bedroom, so I have to sit outside to get the internet (I am really looking forward to winter). Linda gets her meals delivered to her room for $7.50 a meal. I have to eat in a room that is separate from the dining room. Linda stole money from a resident and confessed to the police. The police said she could make payments to the victim. When I break the law I go to jail or a state hospital. Linda has three different cell phones with three different numbers. I was supposed to get a cell phone free; the ILS worker applied for one but it never appeared. My phone will not connect to the Columbia Heights police, the common entry point (to report maltreatment of a vulnerable adult), or to The Traveler so I can escape this madhouse.

As I am writing poems for the Artability Art Show, the light fixture crashes to the floor, shattering into a thousand pieces in front of me (attempted murder?). I was expecting things to happen; it's only going to get worse. Linda has Metro Mobility to get around the cities; my psychiatrist won't do the paperwork so I can receive this service. I have to walk or take the bus, or be hauled around by a social worker (I once drove a '68 Corvette with T-tops —it rattled the windows when I pulled into the garage). I want a Minnesota court ruling so the laws can be changed and the lives of mentally ill people be improved. I am not sure what Linda wants (I have a sneaking suspicion she wants me to give up). I did a background check on A.K.A. Linda Hoover (that's not her real name), and she has been all over the country. I have lived in Minnesota my whole life.

C. GRABER

SLEEP
Poetry

The whole day depends on this fragile sliver of sleep— a destination so hard to reach, and so hard to return from.

My night mind races away from some danger, restless, rhyming, uneasy, struggling finally into dreams.

My morning body is a turtle warm inside its shell of blankets, and I can no more leave this bed than a turtle could leave its shell.

WENDY GREENHAW

ECHOES IN THE SOUL
Poetry

There's a stillness in the soul
A quiet harbor to embrace,
Hidden are its treasures
Life's mysteries are its treasures
Beneath it's quiet stillness
Echoes can be heard,
The silent stillness raging as life's tapestry unfurls
Heartache, pain and sorrow,
Echo in the soul,
A ripple out effect of unkindness we all know.
At times it calls so loudly,
Tears fill the deep dark hole

And drip within the stillness In the Echo of My Soul.
Beyond the pain and sadness,
Most often shared with none
There is a quiet healing if we face it and don't run.
When the silent stillness beckons,
And you find yourself alone,
Just lean into the stillness
Of the Echoes of Your Soul.

Nonfiction

For a brief 14-years, before she was taken by breast cancer, my mother was my greatest teacher and mentor. Her many lessons were passed on to me and I have taught my children and grandchildren. She may not have won the battle, but she did win the race.

My mother was my greatest teacher and mentor in life. She taught me to love all people, despite their differences-that is what made them unique. Her wisdom taught me to embrace not only their uniqueness, but mine.

On cultures, she taught me to seek understanding of all the cultures of the world, without judgement. She taught me not to fear cultures that I didn't understand, but rather study our differences. No one culture is superior over another. We were all created by One. Seek instead to understand the Creator was her wisdom.

On honesty, in all ways and always, be truthful. Truth is your armor.

On religion, she took me to temples, synagogues, Basilicas and Cathedrals to name a few. She taught me to sit silently in them and look closely at the wonders of each. From the arts and paintings, to the music and styles of worship. She taught me there was but One Creator, but so many ways to worship Him. She taught me not to fear evil, knowing my Protector has me under the Shadow of His Wings, and would always be more powerful. She taught me not to "invite" evil into my life, simply be aware of its presence, and look to my Protector when it arrives. She taught me to look at the differences, to seek understanding, but not to allow it to separate me from my Creator. She taught me instead to, "Love all people, in all ways, always."

On beauty, she taught me that the greatest beauty lies within the heart of another. It is a beauty that is pure and unadorned. It was the secret to her own beauty. She taught me the secret to true beauty is to let it shine from inside to the outside, and stand on its own. She taught me to feed that beauty, not with worldly things, but instead with purity and truth. She taught me, "In all ways, and always, be true to yourself and let your heart lead."

On the world, she taught me that no matter where I may walk, in the world, to always leave the places I have been in a better state, as I pass by, then when I came. She taught me to let my "mark" be peace. She also taught me these simple things I could do to make it so:

Nonfiction

Is conflict inevitable? We have inherited survival responses to problems other people give us -- coping with other people by flight, flight or verbal assertiveness. These are primitive survival behaviors: How we become so aggressive or tend to avoid other people, our verbal problem-solving ability, the unique difference between us and other animal species. How learning to feel anxious, ignorant and guilty as children can make us passive, manipulate, and nonassertive as adults. Can parents control their children's behavior without making them feel anxious, ignorant, or guilty?

Our prime assertive human right – how other people violate it. How we are manipulated into doing what others want. Assertive Right I: You have the right to judge your own behavior, thoughts, and emotions, and to take responsibility for their initiation and consequences upon yourself.

How can we stop being manipulated by other people? The manipulator's basic tool: external structure. Need there be rules to cover every situation? Three ways to simplify how you look at your relationship with anyone else, commercial, authority, and equal interactions.

Our everyday assertive rights – the common ways other people manipulate us.

A WORK OF ART

Nonfiction

Michelangelo, the famous Italian sculptor, painter, architect, and poet of four hundred years ago, is reported to have made the statement, "As the marble wastes, the sculpture grows." This statement not only applies literally to the development of a piece of sculpture, but also abstractly to the psychological and spiritual development of our children, which are a work of art.

2. Leave a campground cleaner than when you came.
3. Never litter, it blemishes the world's beauty.
4. Be kind, and let your heart speak, not your tongue.
5. Approach life and people with humility.
6. Walk softly and with purpose. Let that purpose leave its own message to the world.
7. Always let the heart lead, take care to guard what flows in and out of it.
8. Take time to be still - for it is then that you will hear the Master's voice. Let His Voice lead, and you simply follow.
9. Life is a circle--what you sow, you shall also reap. And what you reap, you may have sown.
10. Be still in nature, let its beauty refill your spirit and speak to your soul. Always be aware of the beauty that surrounds you and learn to appreciate it. Nature is an amazing thing--take the time to truly appreciate its wonder.

On love...she taught me it is the Greatest Gift of all. She taught me to learn to speak its many languages, in order to master it. She taught me to let it shine on its own, and in its own way. She taught me, it was the greatest gift I had to give another, and the greatest gift I could ever receive.

On pain, she taught me that the tender side of me, is not a place to share with just anyone. She taught me to be careful, where I share my Pearls (pain). She also taught me to learn not to carry it alone. She taught me there are a few that are capable of carrying it with you, if you only let them. She taught me never to allow another person to hurt me with my own pain, or use it against me to tap into my fears and insecurities.

My mother was the greatest single Teacher in my life. I love her, and I miss her deeply. She was truly the most amazing woman I have ever met. She taught me more in 14 short years, than most people learn in a lifetime about life. I thank God, that at the times she gently poured herself into me, she had the wisdom to know my heart was ready to receive her teachings. Most importantly, she did it not with lectures, but with actions......I love you Mom. Thank you.

...us une ched and the lonely even the rich and the sick
All are welcome who can control their tongue
As well as the good, the bad, the poor, even the slick

As long as they come seeking peace it doesn't
matter from where they come; the north,
the south, the west or the east
They can still participate in the deeds of peace

All are welcome to share a warm meal and a hot drink
During the cold months of the year
And a cool repast in the hot summer season without fear
You should come too if it's peaceful thoughts that you think

We can all share food, chit chat, art sessions and an open library
You will find community support and friendships.
There we will also find the joyful singing of human canaries.
This house is a loving and caring place to feel good and merry.

Helpful hands and strong shoulders to lean on are at this house
You may find an open ear
Eager to hear your thoughts
Or you may receive an encouraging word to hear

This meeting spot is often a peaceful place to
go to just get out of the house
It was built on the foundation of earlier efforts
Of the people in the neighborhood

This program was designed to help make this house
A nexus of community unity
A portal of peaceful interactions
Between the people who live with the city

It is a socially declared zone of peace
I.E. the proverbial holy ground of group acceptance
One of the watering holes of fellowship, and may it stand forever
As one of the local towers of diversity and peace

AMEN, AND HALLELUJAH, MY FRIENDS!

Poetry

Challenged by Society and burdened with their lies,
I hide behind this Mask I wear as a person in disguise.

Judgements rule the truth, and the stigma is unfair.
Criticized and shamed, and so, this mask I wear.

Family, friends and those I love, are cruelest to my heart, so,
safely I retreat away the mask is now my part.

It's fear that makes me feel this way, and unsupported tears.
But, today I have grown tired of this mask that I have worn for years.

The fear imposed by others holds no value in my eyes,
So, I cast aside their untrue words, and shed the ugly lies.

No longer does the mask I wore have purpose in my life.
No longer is the fear allowed to rule my days with strife.

The fear will fuel the fire to outgrow the stigma cast.
The time has come to face those fears and life is mine at last.

Health is not the person but a journey theirs to bear,
Support the ones you know to help them shed the Mask they wear.

I will hold my head up high and speak for those without a voice.
Mental health is but an illness and one that's not our choice.

CHRISTOPHER L. JACKSON

LOIS LANE WILL NEVER BE IN METROPOLIS
AGAIN – 4 MARGOT KIDDER
Poetry

I fear there's nothing left 4 me they say i'm acting selfishly, but if they
knew what would they know that it was all a show and I can't stay here
after u go because the city will never hold as the streets can never speak
those stories told and now it's time 4 my legend 2 come 2 an end cuz Lois
will never be in metropolis again

Many direct services, such as, temporary storage lockers
Entertainment programs, theater, live music.
They also have job training, social service referrals and
you can get your mail delivered there.
At 9:30 am they serve a healthy snack it's usually good food too!

Once a week soul care, foot care program
Show-up to help the poor and homeless
who have sore or hurting feet.

Every now and then they have a bike repair workshop
A cool spot to be if you need help taking back your life
Or even if you're trying to recover
from your bout with strife

But please waste not this chance so nice for
opportunity may not knock twice.
Hey, if you don't make the attempt to grasp the
opportunity to better yourself,

When the possibility presents itself
then it will pass you by but then
don't complain about it.
Because you failed to be about it.

Just do a better job next time.
Because opportunity is always coming and going
So come on lets enter the portal of opportunity together
Where we can find fellowship and good conversation.

Even share some humor, kindness and concern
While networking and data sharing information
That may help someone succeed with their plans to
successfully enter Opportunity's Door.

THE HOUSE THAT PEACE BUILT
Poetry

In the heart of the city
Where crime and hopelessness is a pity
Stands a house amidst the chaos of urban life
It is open to the public and inviting you to seek a better life

Opportunity is a Portal
"i.e. A window or door
A phrase shift of time,
Where you may enter to become more

Possibly find a way to improve your lot in life.
A place for new horizons to start,
Beyond: your present strife.
You might find yourself in a position to grow your smarts

May be able to step back from your problems
And begin to look at your part in the confusions
In order to get a view on
How to march on with your solutions

The catholic charities opportunity center
is such a place providing services for the
poor and homeless, where you can pick
up your pace

They have services to help you clean up
and wash the dirt from your face.
There you can find a bed for the night
through the shelter network system,

And catch some sleep, then wake-up in the morning
take a shower\shave\brush your teeth
Used to be named branch#3 but now it's the O.C (the opportunity center)
You can wash your clothes in their laundry room,

And then look into the mirror and watch your hygiene bloom
You might even find yourself cleaning up your shoes while
buffing up the rest of your survival tools.
Maybe you can get help with housing or finding A Job.

On some days you can get legal advice or even talk to a local judge
Also, while you are there, you can join the lunch line for a free bite to eat
Then if you like to read, maybe grab a book from the library on the wall
It will expand your conversations and help you stand tall

There was a flower growing
On the west side
And as it grew she walked along her streets
And what she saw she knew
It should not be this way
And in her mind an angel writes their notes
2 pass along 2 the child
And as she walked along her streets
She sang frightful words and made heartbreaking beats
And then the police started to shake in fear
They knew their bullets could not stop her
Once everyone hears
And as she walked along her streets
Sne saw the beauty everyone tried to deny
And they accused her of spreading terrifying lies
About words and books and art and bugs and science
And the mayor told her 2 shut up
And the swat team came in the name of justice
And she kept speaking
And the judges hurled sentences
And she held black boys by the hand
Teaching them what they could do
And she gave the black girls brushes and blueprints
And there was a final warning
With threats of Jesus and a nuclear strike on Chicago
And she was kind to little black babies and sat there with them
And buildings fell
And she said she loved a boy because he made her laugh
And Russia declared war and Israel called for sanctions on Chicago
And all of this because she knew it would all be better
Than what it is or what it was
And she walked along her streets on the west side of Chicago
Smiling every time a song played on any radio Satellites fell because she
wouldn't stop
And we didn't want her to. It all needed 2 fall away...

RUN

Poetry

2 those people
When u feel annoyed
Run 2 dem people
Run 2 dem people
When ya wanna kill a black boy
Run
All ya gotta do is run
2 those people when u on dat bullshit
Run 2 dem people
When ya nigga puppy won't sit
Run 2 those people wit ya minority report
Run 2 dem people when ya wanna
Humiliate him in court
Run 2 dem people cuz u got a point 2 prove
Run 2 those people cuz he got
Everything 2 lose
Run 2 dem people cuz his color is dark
Run 2 those people cuz u lack the heart
To treat a man like a man
Cuz you ego won't hold up when u
Testify on the stand
Run 2 dem people cuz this nigga Fuckin up yo plans
It's supposed to be a hoe summer
But dis goofy think he yo man
Run 2 those people when ya need a court order
Cuz ya baby daddy just found out u abusing his daughter
All because he refused 2 glorify
Well u gon show him
Cuz that blue and red light show
Never fails 2 terrify
And when he's locked up nobody can call u on yo lies.
Run 2 dem people when a nigga is stupid enough 2 argue Run 2 dem
people when u tell that man they came here 4 U Run....run....run....
All ya gotta do is....
All ya gotta do is
Run 2 dem people when u can't stand rejection
Run 2 dem people when ya married fucked a black dude and didn't use
protection
Run 2 dem people just save yo reputation
Run 2 dem people
When it's time to get grimy and bring home the bacon.
Run

Like a community lighthouse

Strategically placed and stationed at the edge of our distress to
help guide those lost in the seas of troubled minds
Land and dock safely at the local bay of resources
where they can get help to recover from the roaring waves

And crashing rocks of their past mistakes,
many are saved and often they come bearing the scars of their ordeals
They might have instances of blackouts and the dry shakes of over indulgences
from trying to drown out their issues in the waters of liquid dismay

Or they could still be tripping from falling out of the chemical sky in which
they tried to flee their own personal failures
Only to realize too late that airplanes and not drugs are the only true way to fly
But once we are rescued by the diligent and friendly staff of Avivo
Recovery Resource

They help us to find our way on the roads of our personal recovery
Where we can learn to rebuild or repair our wrecked or lost lives
Some of us will have to go thru a period of Dry-Dock called treatment
To remove the mussel and parasites of negativity from our past errant
journeys that may still be hitchhiking and clinging to the hulls of our lives

These hangers-on are threatening to drag us back into the maelstrom of relapse
I thank the day that I saw the light of hope from the lighthouse
Shining beyond the squalling hurricane of my own misguided choices
These bad decisions caused me to crash my ship of dreams

On the reef rocks of cause and effects, but the (AVIVO RECOVERY
RESOURCE DROP-IN CENTER) is a place where I can find a moment of
clarity, peace, and calm
A comforting place to run to when I need shelter from the recurring and
sometimes lingering storms of my past voyages into despair

My lighthouse of hope is a safe place for me to reflect and take a time-out
in-order to navigate a path that leads to a more responsible plan, one that
directs me to a better bearing in life
And on the day of my recovery, the outreach team used the safety nets of
the local resources

To haul me out of the toil moil of homelessness and set me on a stern
course to regain my sanity, like the coast guards of mental health and for
this I thank you guys for saving me!

Run 2 dem people when it's time 2 turn a profit
Run cuz blue is the color of conscience
Run 2 them people cuz you've fuckin lost it

PHILISTIA JAMES

4 HOURS
Fiction

Everyone knows how dangerous exploring an old abandoned building can be. You don't know who or what you will find. 4 teen urban explorers found this out first hand when they decided to explore an asylum that had been abandoned for over 50 years. Bradly Michaels, James Adams, Daniel Seth and Ethan Wright loved walking through old buildings. Looking at the history of the building in person was better than seeing the pictures on the computer. It had been 3 months since they explored an old building; they were just itching to find a new location to go to. Their teacher, Tod Almond, told them about the old asylum on the edge of town: "Nobody goes there! It's far too dangerous for you boys! I only told you because I thought you would like to hear the history of it, not so you could go there and get killed! Promise me you won't go to that building!"

The boys gave a false promise, and the very next day they headed out to the building. It took them an hour to get there; they only had 4 hours before sunset. They decided they would try to see as much of the building as possible within those 4 hours. As they walked through the building, the stench of mildew filled the air. Old hospital gowns, medical tools and even blood could be seen everywhere. By now they had been in the building for an hour. As they moved upstairs, they were stopped by a large metal door. It looked inviting, so they tried to open it.

After realizing it was stuck, one of the boys, James, climbed into the balcony on his left and was able to get into the room. The darkened room lit up as James pushed open the French doors and he could see nearly everything. His friends asked: "Did you get in? What do you see?" Before they could ask another question, Bradly, Daniel and Ethan heard James let out a terrifying scream.

"HELP! HELP ME HELP! ETHAN, BRAD HELP! GET OFF ME! HELP ME, PLEASE HELP!" Ethan rushed to get out onto the balcony, and get into the next room.

Once Ethan was able to enter the other room, the scene in front of him left him speechless. Ethan watched as a group of what looked like old

---

How could she have disappeared so fast? Where did she go? And, why couldn't they find her? James kept looking at the windows of the houses, hoping she was playing a joke. After looking in a few different houses, James saw Drucilla staring down at him. Her eyes filled with tears and terror; James began running toward that house.

Crush saw James running and asked if he had found her, James told Crush he did as the two ran into the house where they found Drucilla in a back room. What the hell was going on? What the hell was happening?

Crush and James asked Drucilla how she got there. She couldn't speak; she was so scared that she couldn't speak. James picked up Drucilla and walked out of the house. Crush asked, "What are you looking at?" James looked at Crush, "Look! It's the missing kids! They're all here!?" Both James and Crush startled, asked each other, "How?" James looked at Crush with tears in his eyes; he knew he couldn't go back and save them; he had to get Drucilla home. Crush looked up at the missing kids once again, "I...I" James knew what Crush was trying to say. "I know, come on we have to go."

James's little sister started yelling, JAMES! JAMES, CRUSH - HURRY, THEY'RE COMING!" Crush looked behind them to see the missing kids running toward them, as if to bring them back.

James looking at the kids, now realizing why they couldn't leave; they were all dead. Tears began to stream down his face; it was as if he could hear them calling out to him. "Come stay with us; we're so alone. James closed his eyes and continued running to his truck. Drucilla, crying uncontrollably, still couldn't speak. James knew why she was crying.

"It's ok Dru, I know you're scared, we are never going back there. And we certainly aren't telling mom about this." All five were quiet while on the ride home, only to speak and make the promise never to tell a soul what happened on White Forest Drive.

WILLIE L. JOHNSON

MY LIGHTHOUSE OF HOPE
Poetry

Within the harbor of recovery and standing stout
on the break water of depression and stress
There lies a beacon of hope sending out rays of illuminations,

room from the balcony. He suddenly yelled. "NO ETHAN, NO! GO, JUST GO, HURRY!" As the mental patients turned their heads toward Ethan, they began rushing towards him, looking at him as if he were their next meal. Ethan rushed to get outside and climbed from balcony to the other. Once he did, he looked behind him to see if there was anyone there.

There wasn't. Ethan told the others: "We...we need to leave now!" Daniel asked: "Where's James?" Ethan looked up at Daniel and Brad, as tears streamed down his face. "They...they ate James!" Ethan, Daniel and Brad ran from the building. All three boys ran all the way home. Ethan was crying all the way home; he could not believe what he had just seen.

THE BUS
Fiction

I got on the bus. I had a doctor's appointment. Nothing special, just a checkup. I sat down next to this guy who was sitting by the window on the left side. He looked like he was in a deep sleep, nothing could wake him up. As I was putting my bag on the floor in front of me, I noticed a stack of money laying in his hand!

I lifted up the money, his right arm jerked and his head fell back revealing his slit throat. Blood began to spill everywhere. I woke up. It was all a dream. I had fallen asleep on the bus. I looked up to see the people in front of me and the people sitting toward the front of the bus staring at me!

Why? I looked to my right, the people across from me were staring at me too! Looking around the bus everyone was staring at me. I was puzzled. I didn't until seconds later. Everyone on the bus...... All of their faces!?

They all had red eyes but their faces: they weren't there?!?! All I could see were their eyes! I turned to look to the left of me, this guy with a slit throat was staring at me. Suddenly he spoke. "Help...me! Help...me"!

WHITE FOREST DRIVE
Fiction

There are some neighborhoods that people tell stories about and they are either a really bad place to go, a bad place to be or a bad place to live. Just like all of the others, our ghostly neighborhood is just as creepy. Many kids disappeared there. The neighborhood was abandoned because of some

live. I don't know all of the details since they keep changing from person to person.

White Forest Drive is up north in Minnesota; it's been abandoned for the past twenty years. Now people tell ghost stories about how they can hear little kids playing in the streets of the neighborhood. Teenagers would dare each other every Halloween. "Go in the neighborhood and stand in the middle of the street for one hour. If you don't come back, we'll know you're dead."

To some teens, this place was a joke, others took it seriously, since kids did actually disappear there. Five teens, Vida Nalavichi, Drucilla Masters, Adeline Michaela, James Michaela and Crush (Adam Worth, James's best friend) drove the four hours up to White Forest Drive one Halloween, the three girls decided to go up there for fun. They needed something to do. Vida, Drucilla and Adeline were best friends and dared each other to do stupid things all of the time. This year would be different.

As Halloween approached, the girls started planning how they would get there. Adeline asked her big brother to take them up there. The girls promised they would pay him once he got them there; James said ok but made them promise that everyone would return safety. The girls decided what they would take and what they would do once they got back to Brooklyn Hall. They thought they had everything planned out. James and his friend Crush (Adam) took the girls up to White Forest Drive. He was very protective of Adeline and her friends. Once they got there, the girls decided who would go first into the neighborhood and who would stand for one hour before returning.

James told them that wasn't part of the plan; he wasn't going to wait for all three girls to stand for one hour each in the center of a deserted neighborhood for three hours. The girls reluctantly agreed, and decided that Drucilla would be the one to go into the center of the neighborhood for one hour, at first everything was fine. Drucilla was ok, the girls, James and Crush could see Drucilla waving her flashlight around so they could see where she was. Although it didn't take long for things to go wrong.

Drucilla was smiling, telling her friends, James and Crush, how stupid she felt just standing there doing nothing. Suddenly, Drucilla's laugh turned into a blood curdling scream. Something was wrong. James began running towards her with Crush running behind him and when they got to the spot where they saw Drucilla standing a few seconds earlier, there was no one there. Her flashlight was rolling on the ground where it fell.